LEARNING RESOURCE CENTRE
The Oxford Academy
Sandy Lane West
Littlemore
Oxford OX4 6JZ

Ransom Neutron Stars
My Toys
by Stephen Rickard

Published by Ransom Publishing Ltd.
Unit 7, Brocklands Farm, West Meon, Hampshire GU32 1JN, UK
www.ransom.co.uk

ISBN   978 178591 437 9
First published in 2017

Copyright © 2017 Ransom Publishing Ltd.
Text copyright © 2017 Ransom Publishing Ltd.
Cover photograph copyright © m-imagephotography
Other photographs copyright © m-imagephotography; mevans; archideaphoto; kanate; Cesare Andrea Ferrari; Georgijevic; mypum; RapidEye; vacl; Apriori1; milosljubicic; Sage78; baona; piovesempre; 3dan3; andreamuscatello.

A CIP catalogue record of this book is available from the British Library.

All rights reserved. No part of this publication may be reproduced, stored in a retrieval system, or transmitted, in any form or by any means, electronic, mechanical, photocopying, recording or otherwise, without the prior permission of the publishers.

The right of Stephen Rickard to be identified as the author of this Work has been asserted by him in accordance with sections 77 and 78 of the Copyright, Design and Patents Act 1988.

Ransom Neutron Stars

My Toys

Stephen Rickard

Ransom

I like my car.

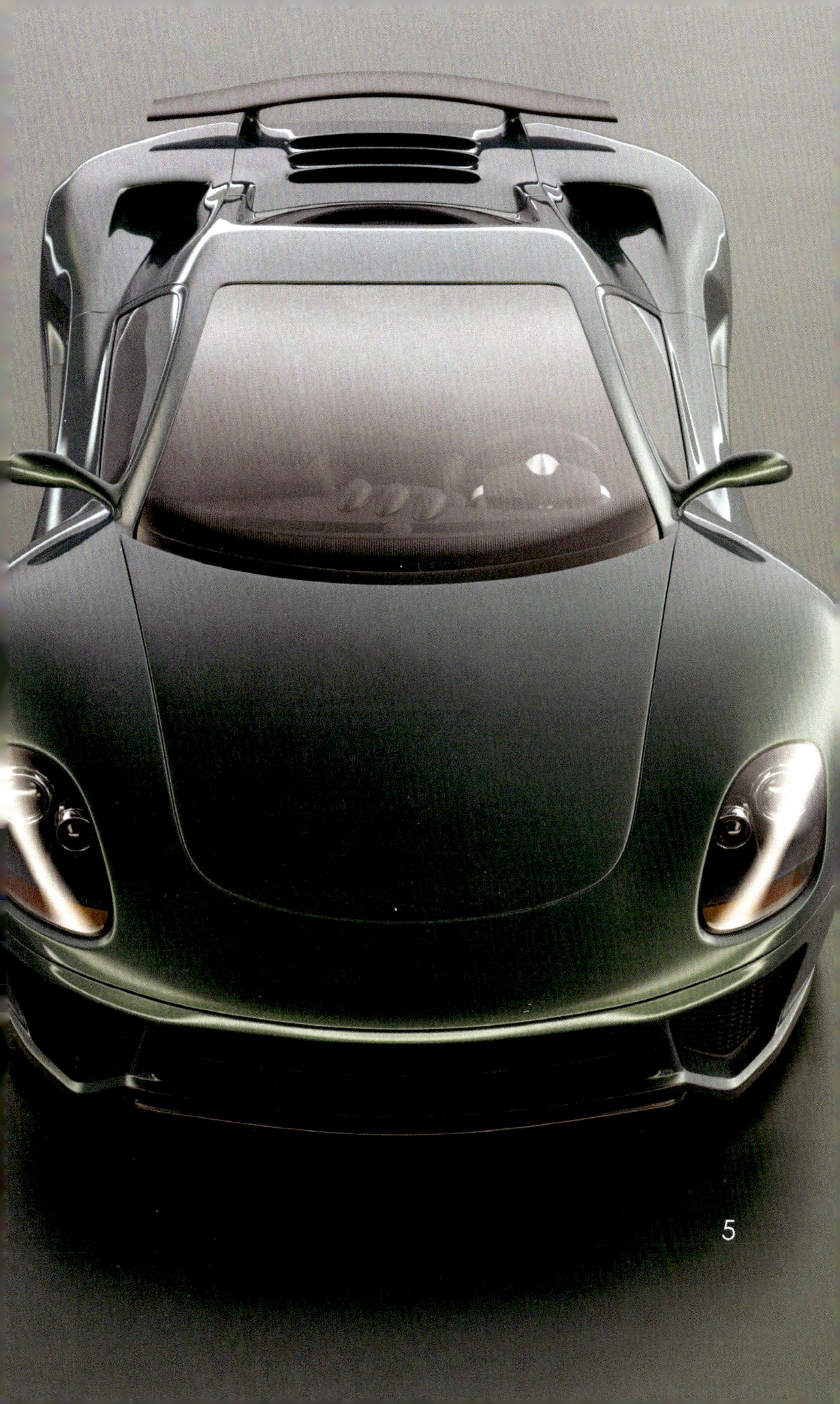

I like my TV.

7

I like my laptop.

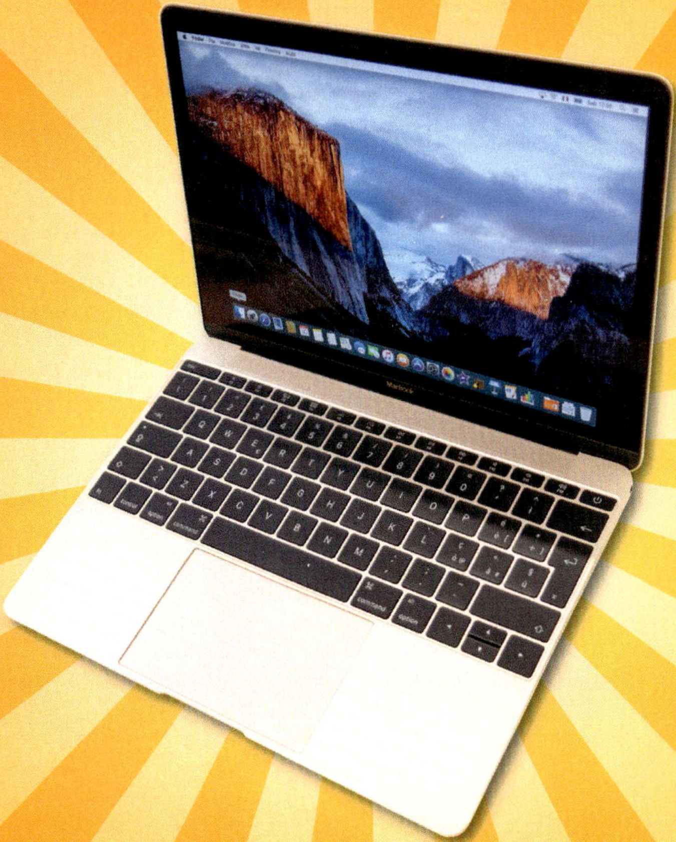

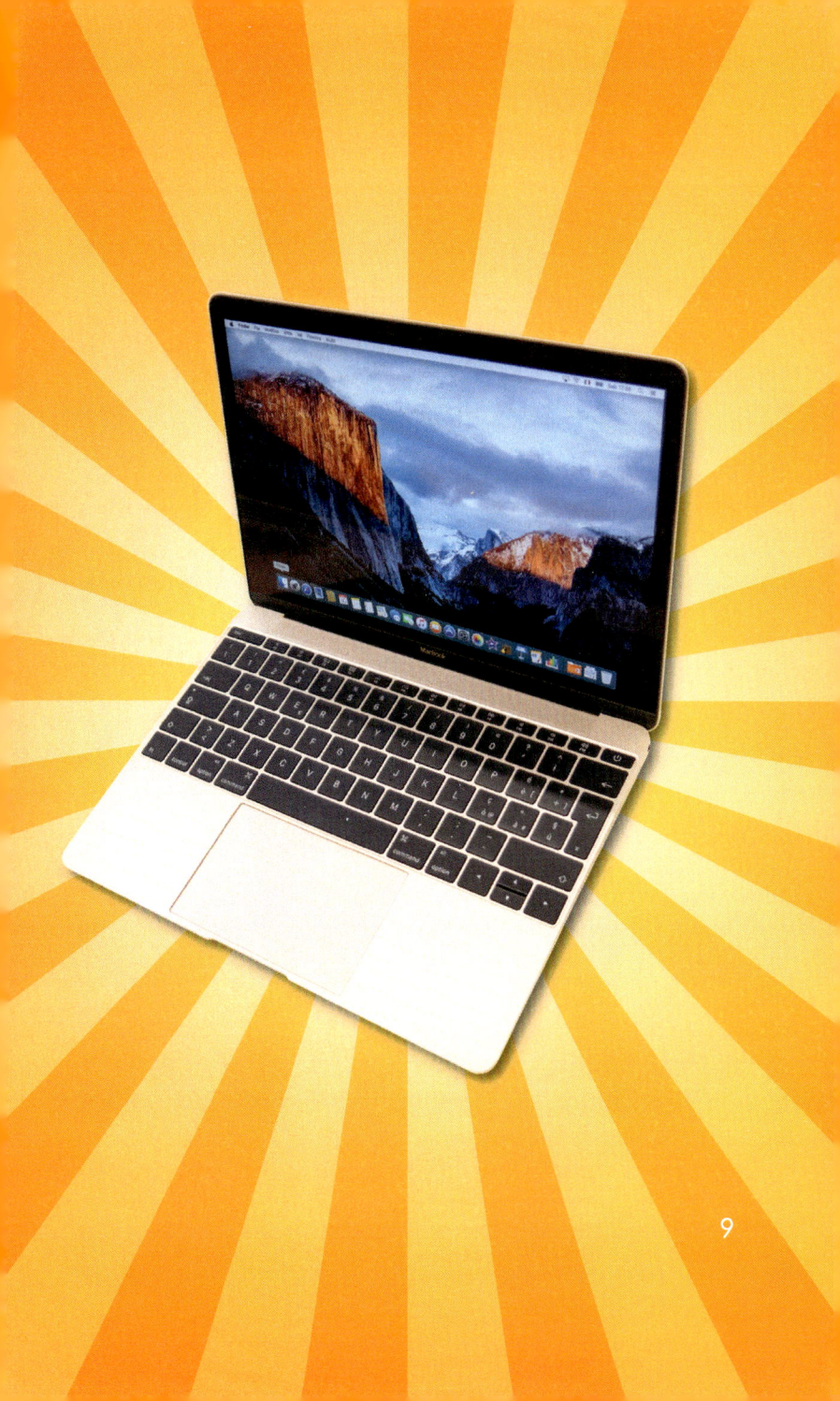

I like my phone.

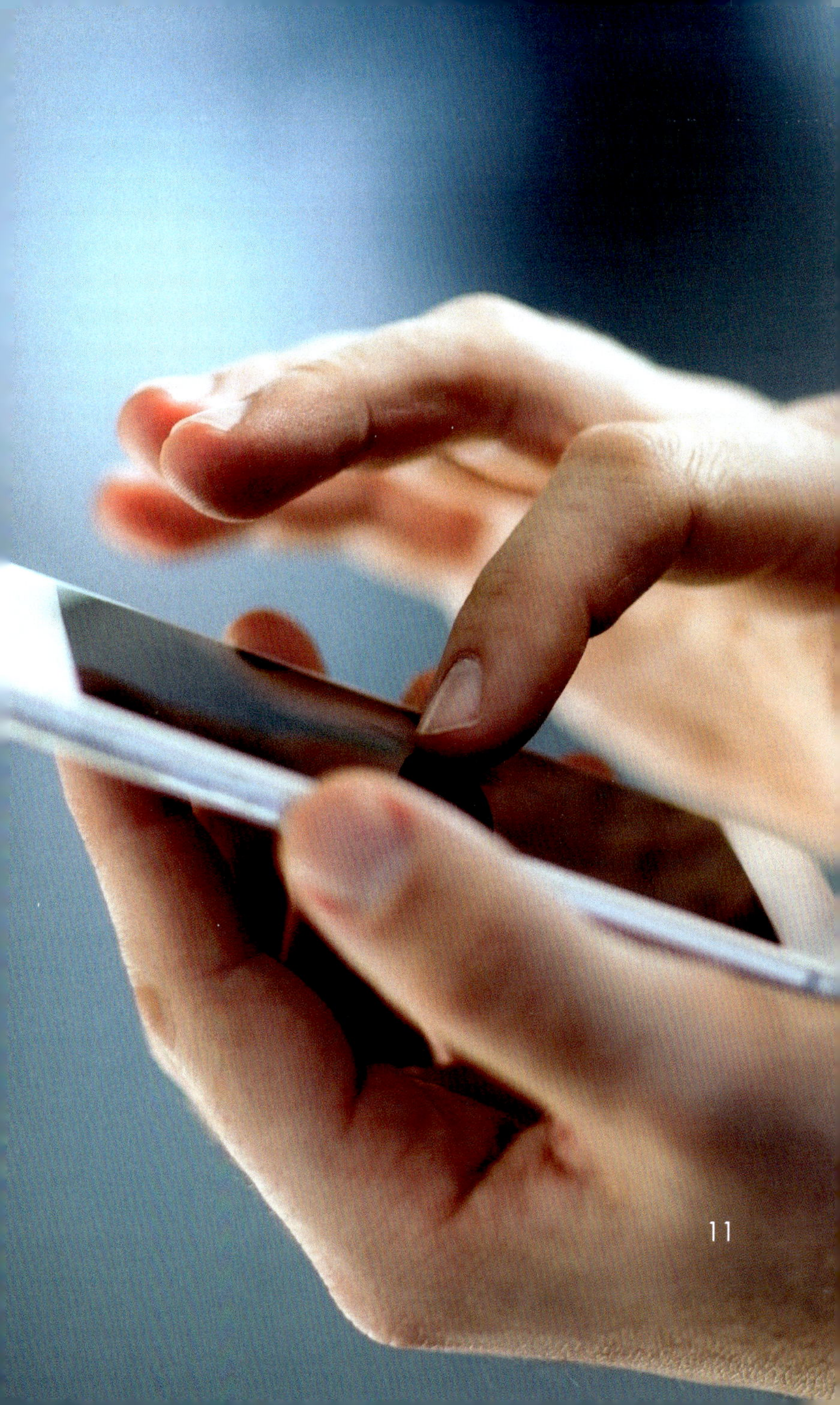

I like my watch.

13

I like my bicycle.

15

I like my camera.

17

I like my drone.

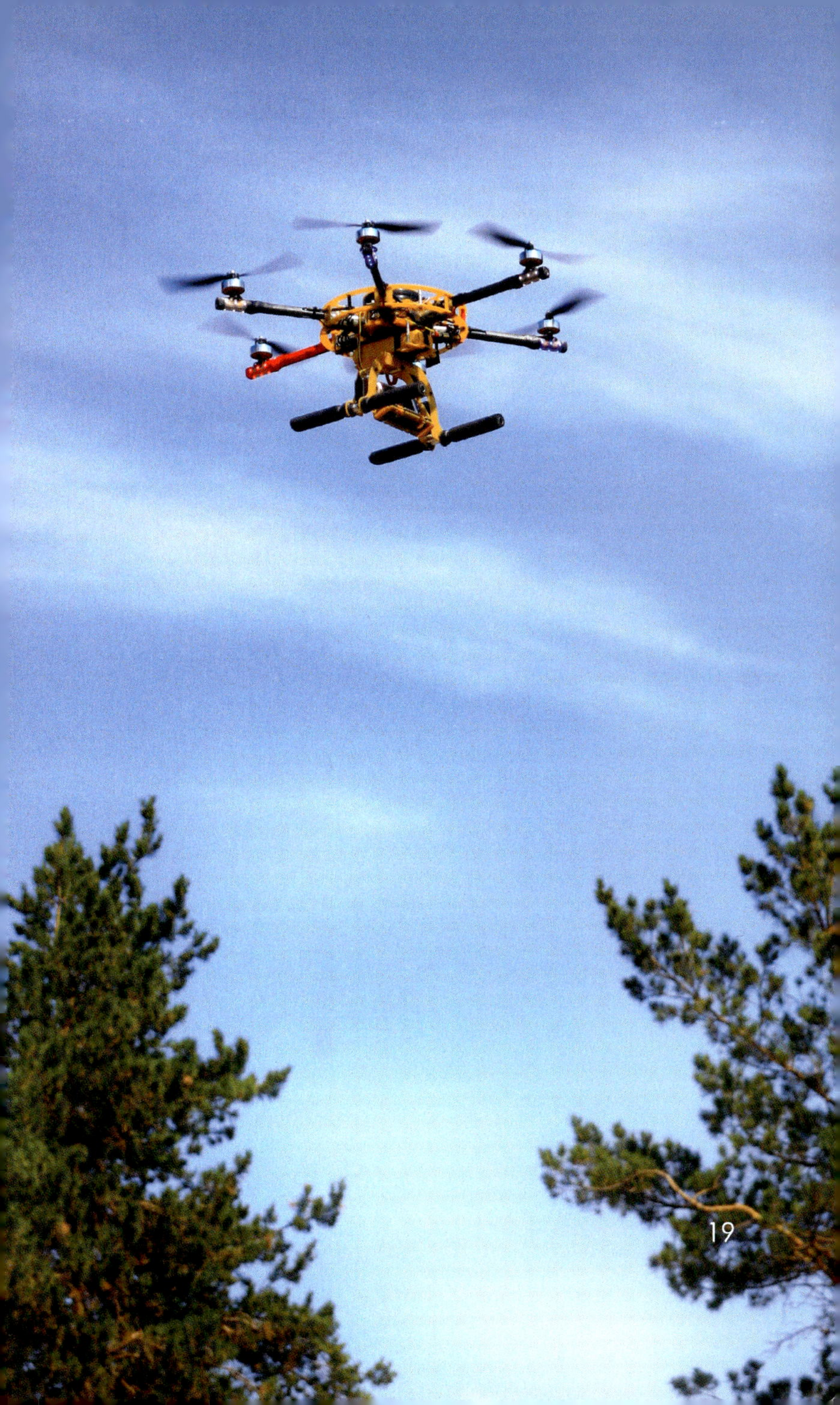

I like my coffee machine.

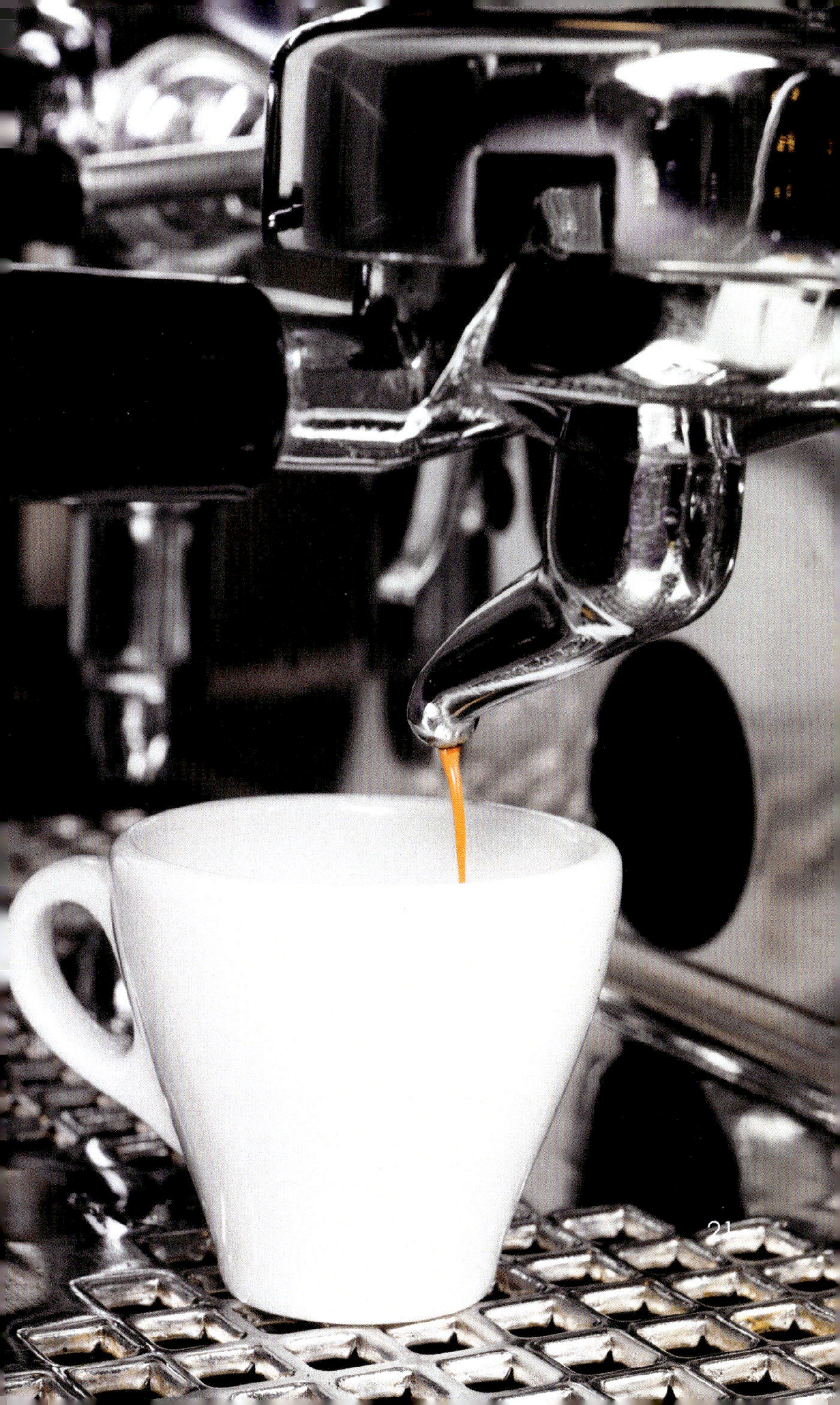

I like my music player.

23

I like my tablet.

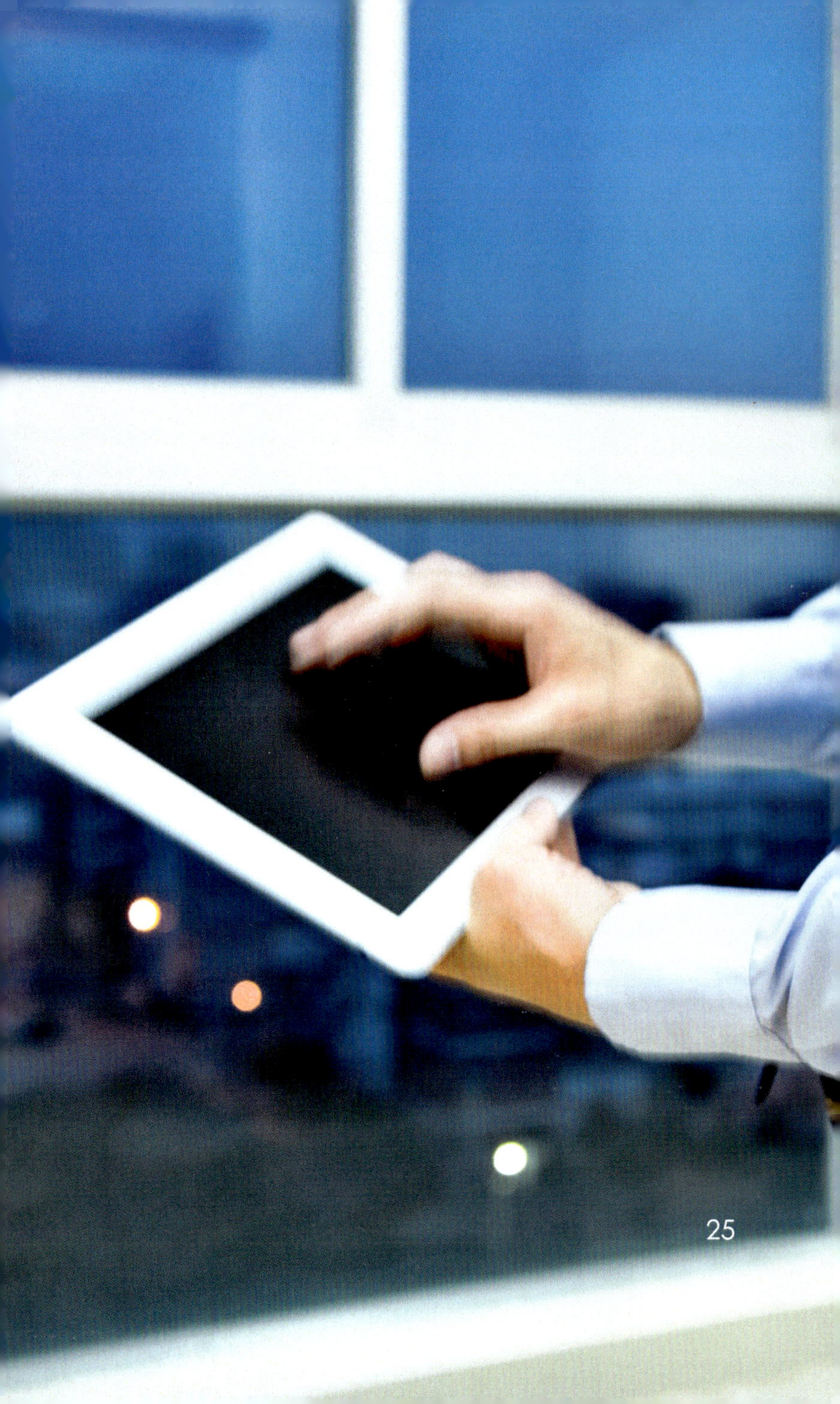

I like my pool.

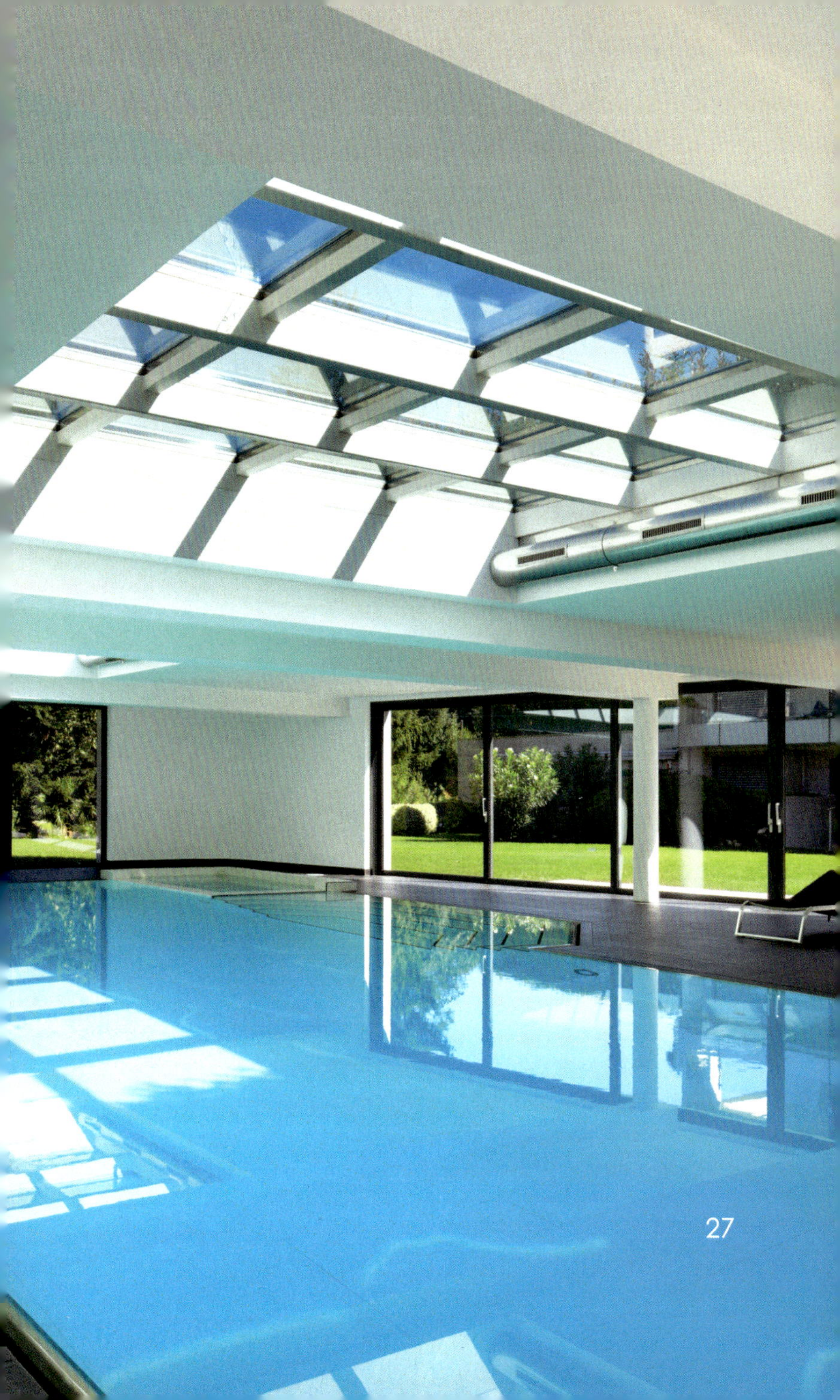

I like my helicopter.

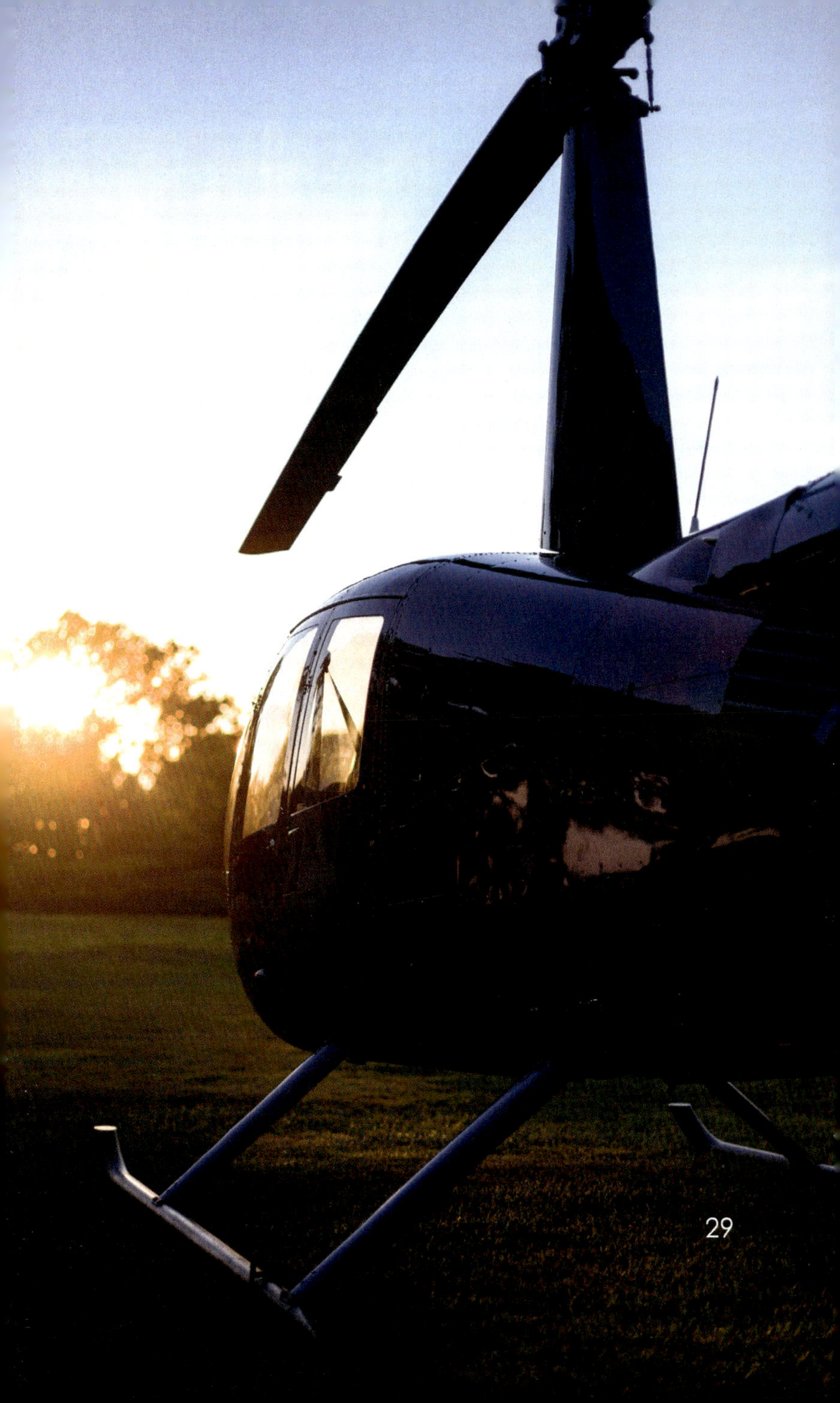

I like my boat.

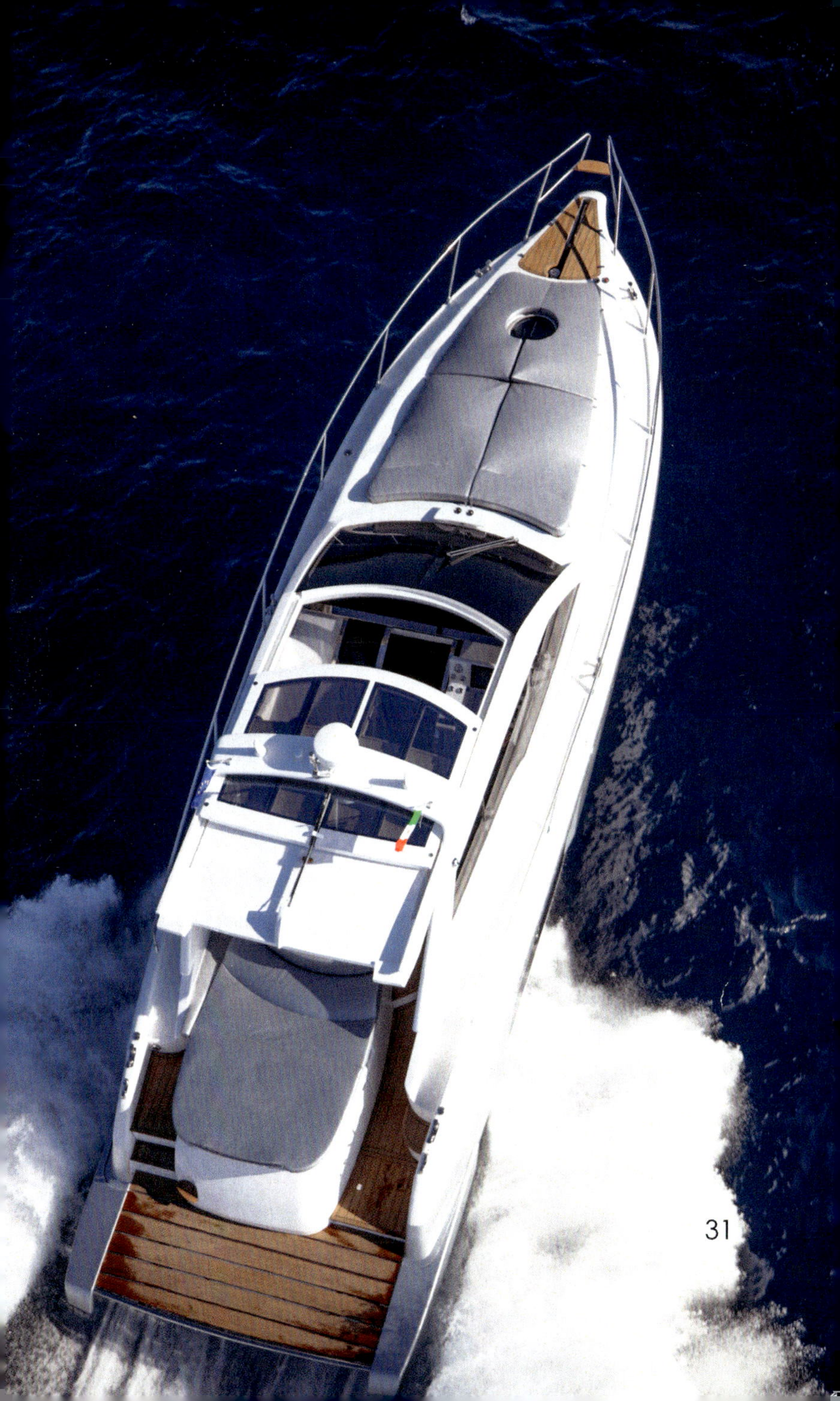

I like my toys.

33

Have you read?

Curry!

by
Cath Jones

Free Runners

by
Alice Hemming

Have you read?

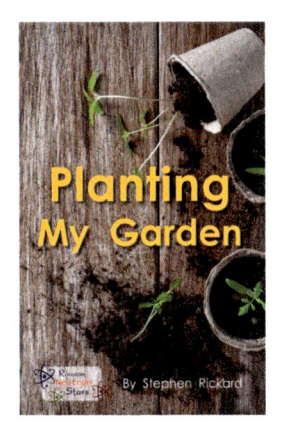

Planting My Garden

by
Stephen Rickard

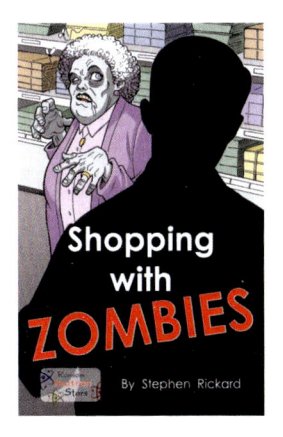

Shopping with Zombies

by
Stephen Rickard

Ransom Neutron Stars

My Toys
Word count **62**

Pink Book Band

Phonics

Phonics 1	Not Pop, Not Rock Go to the Laptop Man Gus and the Tin of Ham	*Phonics 2*	Deep in the Dark Woods Night Combat Ben's Jerk Chicken Van
Phonics 3	GBH Steel Pan Traffic Jam Platform 7	*Phonics 4*	The Rock Show Gaps in the Brain New Kinds of Energy

Book bands

Pink	Curry! Free Runners **My Toys**	*Red*	Shopping with Zombies Into the Scanner Planting My Garden
Yellow	Fit for Love The Lottery Ticket In the Stars	*Blue*	Awesome ATAs Wolves The Giant Jigsaw
Green	Fly, May FLY! How to Start Your Own Crazy Cult The Care Home	*Orange*	Text Me The Last Soldier Best Friends

LEARNING RESOURCE CENTRE
The Oxford Academy
Sandy Lane West
Littlemore
Oxford OX4 6JZ